# The Poetic Ramblings of a Colorado Native

Monica Yoknis

This book is dedicated to Esther Brown, my dear pen pal who has been encouraging me to publish these for years. Thanks, Esther.

Copyright © 2017 by Monica Yoknis
All rights reserved.

ISBN: 978-0-692-93010-6

# Whispers in the Forest
April 2006

The wind passes its secrets though the trees.

The trees whisper their secrets to the wind.

I hear them.  The pines whisper, the aspens laugh.

What secrets do the trees know? What stories does the wind tell?

I wonder as I sit in the forest.  I don't understand the trees or the wind, but I enjoy

Listening to the whispers in the forest.

# Spring?
April 29, 2006

Is it Spring?

I see flowers!

I smell their sweet perfume!

Leaves are emerging on trees.

The grass is turning green.

It certainly feels like Spring!

Then why is it snowing?!

I drive down roads lined with budding trees.

White flakes pass through the beams of my headlights.

I encounter a blizzard!

But wait.

White flakes are not snow.

I'm driving through a blizzard of white petals!

Flowering trees surround me.

I savor the sweet scent.

Yes, Spring is here!

# My Beloved Columbine
June 16, 2006

Blue as the sky.

White as the snow.

Higher you lift me as I follow you there.

To the mountain meadow you take me.

To the place where Earth and Sky are one.

I find you growing tall and beautiful,

My beloved Columbine.

8

# Grandpa
July 19, 2006

Who is Grandpa?

Mom's dad?

Old man?

Wise elder?

Yes, Grandpa is all these things.

But Grandpa is also so much more

Grandpa is a stately elk.

Grandpa is a noble eagle.

Grandpa is a wise old mountain.

Grandpa is all those stories of times long ago.

Grandpa's stories prove that mom was once a kid.

Grandpa's stories make us realize that there was a world before us.

Who is Grandpa?

Grandpa is a treasure for all who come after.

Grandpa may have left us, here.

But don't be sad.

Grandpa is soaring with eagles, roaming with elk, and sitting high on mountain tops.

Grandpa is always with us, in spirit and in our memories.

So think of Grandpa often, and he'll live for eternity.

# The Deception of Distance
July 28, 2006

I finally found it.

That piece of myself I lost so long ago.

I found it at the top.

I'd scattered myself.

So far away from myself, I was.

But one piece was missing.

Where can I find this piece?

Where did I leave it?

This piece that holds me together.

I found it at the top.

At the top, I can see all of me.

All those pieces I scattered.

I can see at the top.

Where are these pieces?

The first piece, the oldest, resides with Long's Peak.

The second piece lives with Denver.

The third piece I gave to Pike's Peak.

The fourth piece I discovered in Leadville.

All points seem so far from each other.

The distances too great to be together at once.

Where is the piece that holds me together?

I found it at the top.

At the top of Mount Evans.

From here I can see all of me.

Here I sit, in the middle.

Long's Peak to the North.

Denver to the East.

Pike's Peak to the South.

And Leadville to the West.

What has seemed so far away,

So scattered,

Is really very close.

I'm not so scattered as I thought.

And that, I find, is the deception of distance.

# **Reality Check**
July 30, 2006

Here I sit, among the trees, and grass, and wild flowers.

I close my eyes and open my ears.

What do I hear?

The constant murmuring of Fall River dominates the sound-scape.

But there's more.

The call of a crow.

The buzz of a fly.

The click, click, click of a grasshopper.

A breeze drifts past me, full of

mountain perfume.

The soothing smell of pines.

The green scent of sun-warmed grass.

The pungent odor of clover.

Upon opening my eyes, I see river, trees, grass and flowers.

But look closer, there's more than the obvious to see.

The stump of an old tree, cut close to the ground.

Sad a tree is dead, but a closer look brings hope.

Mushrooms rise out of the wood.

Moss and lichen are forming a carpet across the stump.

And there, on the edge, grows a baby tree.

Life is all around us, always.

All we have to do is take a few moments to notice it.

Never mind how you feel.

Pause a moment to find out what you feel.

Then you can know, this is life.

# **Distant Thunder**
July 30, 2006

Is there any more perfect way

To end a Summer day

Than with the sound of distant thunder?

I have to wonder,

As I hear it rumble

Across the mountain sides.

The day draws to its end,

I decide,

As I listen with all my heart

To the sound of Distant Thunder.

# The Greatest Offering
August 30, 2006

Meat and Wine

Beer and Bread

Why should I shed

A tear for You?

"Because, My dear,

It is you!"

# Gold Rush
September 17, 2006

Gold.

"Gold?"

Yes, there's gold in them thar hills!

"Where?"

Look high in the mountains.

The higher you go, the more you will find.

But go soon, before it's gone.

"Gone?"

Yes, all things must end.

But don't worry.

If you miss it this year, there's always the next.

"Next year?"

Of course, every year about this time,

There's gold on every hillside,

And the sounds of clashing rams, bulls, and bucks fill the air.

This is the Colorado Gold Rush,

When the aspens change from emerald to gold.

"The Gold Rush!

It's Colorado or Bust!"

# The Mountain's Day
October 3, 2006

Under Winter's sparkling blanket sleeps the Mountain through the night.

Spring's bright morning wakes the Mountain, seeing flowers bright.

All through Summer's fine warm day, the Mountain watches as we play.

As Autumn's evening falls, the Mountain yawns in reds and golds.

Winter's shining blanket covers the Mountain once again, and soon a new day will begin.

# The Death of a Friend
October 19, 2007

In a gust of wind, Summer's last breath.

Green lost is yellow given,

Then blown away by Summer's last breath.

All warmth lost,

As darkness descends.

We huddle together waiting for the light,

Waiting for the warmth,

As we mourn the death of our friend, Summer.

# The Pink Veil
November 29, 2007

Above the pure mantle of white

Drapes the gossamer veil of pink.

Blushing faces shine demurely though the haze.

The veil, is it falling or rising?

I cannot say.

The light grows stronger, the pink veil brightens.

The mantle flashes with bright pink light.

The veil turns from pink to yellow.

Blushing faces disappear behind

the now solid veil.

The sun has risen.

The mountains retreat behind their veil of blowing snow.

# **Tumble On**
December 4, 2007

Ah, the Tumbleweed!

Rolling, bouncing, dipping, and dodging.

Where the wind blows, so the Tumbleweed.

The poignant, iconic Tumbleweed,

Where would the American West be without you?

Crosser of highways,

Clogger of fences,

Our beloved,

Perfect (if prickly),

Ubiquitous Tumbleweed.

Tumble on, Tumbleweed, tumble on!

# **My Darling Peaches**
August 15, 2015

Oh, my dear Peaches,

Fluffy and fair,

How long are your ears,

How brown your eyes.

Sweet Bunny of mine,

How loving your gaze,

Your kisses so gentle,

My pain you always ease.

So, my darling fuzzbutt,

I will love you always,

I'll tickle your pouf,

And cuddle your fur.

Lovely Peaches, my bun,

You've saved me from sorrow,

Thank you dear bunny,

My heart is always yours.

# **My Peaches, My Heart**
August 10, 2017

Soft and round, my Peaches.
Sweet and fuzzy, my Peaches.
Warm and loving, my Peaches.

Sad and lonely, my heart.
Empty and hurting, my heart.
Dark and defeated, my heart.

My Peaches comforts my heart.
My Peaches fills my heart.
My Peaches lightens my heart.
My Peaches, my heart.

www.ingramcontent.com/pod-product-compliance
Lightning Source LLC
Chambersburg PA
CBHW031430290426

44110CB00011B/602